W9-AQV-732

HEALING
BURNOUT

A JOURNAL TO FIND PEACE AND PURPOSE

CHARLENE RYMSHA

ROCK
POINT
QUARTOKNOWS.COM
NEW YORK, NY

CONTENTS

Introduction

Life doesn't have to be so hard. We as humans are very good at over-complicating life. In fact, our evolved brains are SO good at thinking that we can think ourselves into anything—but thinking ourselves out of jams gets tricky and can lead to burnout.

Burnout is the culmination of a depletion of internal resources due to chronic and ongoing stress, leaving you tired, despondent, and joyless. I often hear it described as mental, emotional, and physical exhaustion. This experience makes total sense, since chronic stress effectively cuts off clear communication between all systems in the body and mind, leading to lowered capacity to function.

Burnout is like thinking ourselves into a corner with no foreseeable way out. So, we keep pushing into that corner, hoping it will eventually budge, all the while feeling more and more exhausted. Yet, if you're willing to take a step back, look around at your options, and apply a different tactic, a new potential is possible.

It's helpful to start by recognizing burnout as your wake-up call to course correct. You didn't choose for your life to feel exhausting or disconnected, yet here you are. The good news is you've simply lost sight of how you truly want to live and who you really are, and this can be remedied, because the answers to how you want to live and who you really are already reside within you. The vibrant, energetic, fun, interesting, passionate, ambitious, driven person that you are still exists—it's just time to deconstruct and reorganize your reality so that it aligns with the best version of you.

I honor you for picking up this journal and making the decision to change. As you work through the exercises within, you can expect to experience growing pains along the way, since true healing requires letting go of the known and stepping into the unknown. The brain gets scared when it doesn't know what to expect; therefore, I designed this journal so that the exercises build upon each other, scaffolding to the next level. As you learn to deeply trust yourself in this process, your perspective will shift from fear to excitement. You're already ambitious and want the best out of life—I can help you get there without the added stress. Now, let's begin your journey to recovery from burnout!

How to Use This Journal

This journal is designed to help you do the deep healing work necessary to get out of burnout and into a state of sustainable well-being. It is a companion to my book *Burn Bright*, which offers a more in-depth guide to healing from burnout. You can use this journal alongside the book to deepen your practice, or on its own as a place to reflect on your experience with burnout and begin the healing process.

In the first section, Healing Burnout, you'll find a series of writing prompts that walk you through the process of recognizing and addressing the symptoms and causes of burnout in your life. You'll begin with mindfulness as a concept and practice and then move on to the body and mind. You'll continue to explore emotions and identify social and personal values. These prompts and exercises are most useful if done in order, as they're meant to build on each other.

The next two sections, Continuing Wellness Plan and Visualizing Future Wellness, are intended to help you maintain the good habits you've learned and keep burnout at bay. The Continuing Wellness Plan section will give you a space to flesh out the practices and habits that you've found most beneficial—there's space to write out multiple plans, giving you the flexibility to adapt as your needs change over time. In the Visualizing Future Wellness section, you'll practice a visualization exercise that will help you to envision and achieve the new life you've been working toward.

Consistency and flexibility are key—so go at your own pace, returning to previous prompts and exercises when needed, and focus on the prompts that are most helpful for you. As you change, so will your practice. This recovery process and the reflections in this book are designed to fit into your already full day, and as you build your daily awareness practice, you'll soon notice that your days will feel less hectic and a lot calmer.

Healing Burnout

Within this section, you'll find writing prompts that will walk you through the process of healing burnout. Reflect on the way burnout manifests in your life, learn to address those symptoms, and heal yourself in mind, body, and spirit.

BURNOUT SYMPTOMS SELF-ASSESSMENT

Begin by taking a look at this checklist of common burnout symptoms, and check off any and all that apply to you. This will help you determine whether, and in what ways, you're experiencing burnout. This isn't an exhaustive list or a diagnostic test, but a self-awareness tool that will help you understand what burnout currently looks and feels like for you.

○ I'm totally exhausted most of the time.

○ I feel overwhelmed by my mounting to-do list and competing priorities.

○ I feel constantly busy, yet I feel like I'm achieving less than I should.

○ I experience anxiety or low-grade panic.

○ I struggle with work-life balance and have little personal time, even for friends and family.

○ I'm becoming increasingly irritable, annoyed, angry, and short-tempered.

○ I'm under a crushing amount of pressure to succeed.

○ I'm increasingly cynical or hypercritical toward myself and others.

○ I have trouble either falling asleep or staying asleep.

○ I find it hard to concentrate and stay on task.

○ Life has become a bunch of tasks to get done, and I'm losing all sense of purpose.

○ I've been drinking and/or eating too much (or perhaps, eating too little).

○ I worry a lot about work, people, and the future and/or the past.

○ I suffer from digestion problems, tension headaches, and/or chronic aches and pains.

Take a moment to reflect on your answers. What symptoms resonate with you? Are there any others you experience that weren't listed here?

YOUR STRESS TRIGGERS

Think about a normal day for you. Start by thinking of the morning as you wake up and mentally walk yourself through your day until you go to bed. What situations bring on stress? Each situation is a stress trigger of yours. Review the following list of common arenas where stress lurks and write down your specific triggers.

At home:

Your commute:

At work:

Friends/family/partner:

_____

_____

_____

_____

Financial:

_____

_____

_____

_____

Social media:

_____

_____

_____

_____

Other:

_____

_____

_____

_____

HANDLING STRESSFUL MOMENTS

~~~~~~

Think of one of the stress triggers you identified on pages 12-13. Here, you'll reflect on how you'll handle this trigger when it comes up in your life, and make a plan for calming yourself.

Describe a situation that's a stress trigger for you:

_____

_____

_____

_____

_____

_____

How does your body feel when this situation comes up? Describe any physical symptoms (e.g. sweaty palms, fast heartbeat, tightness in the stomach):

_____

_____

_____

_____

_____

_____

_____

Write down a few ways you'll be able to recognize this stress trigger next time:

_____

_____

_____

_____

_____

_____

Brainstorm a few methods you can use to begin calming yourself in this situation. What can you say to yourself in the moment to counteract the stress or fear you feel?

_____

_____

_____

_____

_____

_____

_____

Try out these methods the next time you're in this situation. How did it go?

_____

_____

_____

_____

RECLAIM YOURSELF

Your nervous system may be in survival mode, but wellness is not mere survival. It's about reclaiming who you are beyond the confines of debilitating stress so that you can truly live. These questions are intended to get your mind thinking about reclaiming who you are. When you think it, you can become it. These answers will provide guidance as you find your way back to who you are and how you want to live.

In what ways does stress cut me off from what I know?

Who am I without stress?

Who would I be if stress could be more contained in my life?

THREE-WORD MANTRA

Mantras are positive statements made in the present tense. As you begin to practice making conscious choices that align with your desired life, try this exercise. Create a short and positive statement that reinforces your sense of personal wellness.

STEP 1: What is one word that would describe the opposite of burnout for you? You can select from the list below or add your own. You can even change it tomorrow, so there's no pressure. Simply pick one now.

○ Ease	○ Rested	○ Bubbly
○ Playfulness	○ Funny	○ Connected
○ Joy	○ Kind	○ Effortless
○ Fun	○ Open	○ Unstoppable
○ Grace	○ Flow	○ Available
○ Light	○ Freedom	○ Grounded
○ Happy	○ Love	○ Carefree
○ Relaxed	○ Simple	○ Peace

Now that you have chosen your one word, add it to this phrase:

I choose _____

STEP 2: Say this mantra to yourself three times right now. How does it feel? You may notice that you're having some resistance to the statement with counter thoughts such as, *No I'm not*, or some other automatic thought reaction. Or maybe you're embracing this experience and feeling the lightness of your mantra. Either way, this is an awareness practice that begins to reinforce your new choice. I encourage you to repeat your simple three-word mantra as often as possible. And as you do, notice how your emotions and body respond. Below, record these responses, and note whether they change over time.

MONOTASKING

Multitasking creates a disorganized brain pattern that scatters your focus. When you practice one task at a time, you gain the basic tenets of mindfulness and retrain your brain back into mental clarity. Follow these steps for just two minutes a day to improve your focus.

STEP 1: Choose any single task that you already perform in a typical day. Examples include making coffee, brushing your teeth, listening to a podcast, etc. Which task will you choose?

STEP 2: Engage in that one activity with full focus. This means you're not scrolling through your news feed while brushing your teeth, checking your email while listening to a podcast, or whatever it may be. Place all of your attention on this one action.

STEP 3: Notice any urge you may feel to reach for something else to do and then return your attention to the one task.

What thoughts or urges came up for you during this exercise?

What felt good about it?

_____

_____

_____

_____

_____

_____

_____

_____

What felt difficult?

_____

_____

_____

_____

_____

_____

_____

_____

ADVANCED MONOTASKING

Once you've practiced the exercise on page 20 and feel confident in your ability to complete it with minimal distractions, try these variations to advance your practice.

Try adding more time to your monotask. How does this change your experience?

Practice this exercise at another point in the day when you notice you're multitasking. The practice would then be to stop everything that you're doing and choose to do only one thing at that time. What thoughts or urges come up for you?

_____

_____

_____

_____

_____

_____

Review your day's to-dos, decide what sequence to perform them in, and do one item at a time. If something unexpected pops up, temporarily suspend what you're doing and give it your full attention. What worked well about this process? What was difficult?

_____

_____

_____

_____

_____

_____

_____

BOOSTING GRATITUDE

The practice of cultivating gratitude allows your body and mind to pay attention to what's working well in your life. To start, think about something or someone you really appreciate. Create a positive statement about that thing or person with "I get to . . ." and fill in the blank. Then, be still with this statement and feel a sense of appreciation. Practice this gratitude exercise as often as you want, because the more you feel it, the more gratitude will become an ingrained part of your life.

What do you appreciate about this thing or person?

_____

_____

_____

_____

_____

I get to _____

How do you feel when you take the time to appreciate it?

_____

_____

_____

_____

_____

What do you appreciate about this thing or person?

I get to

How do you feel when you take the time to appreciate it?

ACTIVATING YOUR VAGUS NERVE

There are different ways to practice mindfulness, but for right now, the important piece is to become aware of what you're doing in the present moment. One way to do this is to focus on your breath, observing as you inhale and exhale. Taking this one step further, you can activate the vagus nerve with a focused breathing technique. The vagus nerve is a large nerve bundle that connects mind and body in a way that triggers the parasympathetic (rest-and-recovery) response in your nervous system.

To activate the vagus nerve, you'll need to slow your breathing down to five to seven breaths per minute, which equates to twenty seconds per breath. Here, it is broken down into three parts per breath: five-count inhale, five-count held breath, and ten-count exhale (5:5:10).

STEP 1: Sit quietly with your eyes closed and focus your attention on your breath.

STEP 2: Start the breathing sequence without the 5:5:10 count as you become acquainted with the rhythm. Do this: inhale, hold, exhale.

STEP 3: Next, with curiosity rather than self-judgment, do your best to breathe in for a count of five, hold for five, and then exhale for ten.

STEP 4: Repeat this breathing rhythm a few more times to the best of your current ability.

STEP 5: Then sit quietly with yourself and notice the thoughts that arise and how your body feels.

STEP 6: Open your eyes to finish this round of the exercise.

How do you feel after doing this exercise?

_____

_____

_____

_____

_____

_____

_____

How does your experience of this exercise change after you've practiced it a few times?

_____

_____

_____

_____

_____

_____

_____

GROUNDED EXPANSION

This exercise is a way to accept your body as a place of strength, rooted like a tree, to provide the basis of feeling confident, alive, and ready to be fully you. After you practice these steps, reflect on how this exercise changes your connection to your body.

STEP 1: Begin by standing with your feet at a comfortable distance apart. With your eyes open, look at your body (standing in front of a full-length mirror is recommended). Look at yourself standing, while you feel your feet planted firmly on the floor. Now feel your feet grounded into the earth, as if they are roots of a tree.

STEP 2: Close your eyes and continue to notice the feeling of your feet rooted into the ground.

STEP 3: From here, stand as tall as possible, without forcing it. Standing tall and rooted, raise your arms out to your sides, extending up at an angle in a "V" formation toward the sky. Remaining as grounded as possible in your feet and lower body, allow for the sense of extension upward through your arms and out your fingertips as if they are tree limbs reaching for the warm sun. Relaxing your shoulders, breathe as you normally would.

STEP 4: Remain here for one to three minutes as you simultaneously feel the anchor of your foothold and your capacity for expansion through your upper body, arms, and fingertips. When your mind wanders, return its focus to your body's current action.

STEP 5: Once complete, release your arms from this position and place one hand on your heart and one on your belly. With eyes closed, notice how both your body and your mind feel in the moment. Then open your eyes, notice your body in the mirror, and return to your day.

How does your body feel after doing this exercise?

_____

_____

_____

_____

_____

_____

_____

How does your mind feel?

_____

_____

_____

_____

_____

_____

_____

_____

MIND-BODY COMMUNICATION

The communication between body and mind is interactive and goes both ways, meaning that the body responds to the mind, just as the mind responds to the messages of the body. Here, you'll practice aligning these two areas by focusing on one, then the other.

First, use your mind to focus directly on what your body is doing in the present moment. For example, if you're eating an ice-cream cone, notice the experience: how you hold the cone, what it tastes like, what it looks like. Record what your mind notices about your body's actions.

Next, shift your attention to your body itself as you continue the same action. If you are eating ice cream, does it feel cold? Are you experiencing a sugar rush? Record what sensations you experience in your body.

How does it feel to take this time to focus on your body?

HEAD-TO-BODY RATIO

The Head-to-Body Ratio is a way to remind yourself to pay attention to your body and mind by asking yourself, *How much of me is living in my head, and how much of me is living in my body, right now?* For example, if you find that most of your awareness is in your thoughts (your head), then a likely numerator would be eighty, and which is very common, then a likely numerator would be eighty, and the denominator would be twenty (the numbers need to add up to one hundred). This is a quick tool to get you acquainted with your body in relation to your mind—try checking in on this ratio three times a day.

STEP 1: Sit quietly for a few moments (eyes can be open or closed) and ask yourself, *How much of me is living in my head, and how much of me is living in my body, right now?*

STEP 2: Remain in quiet observance as the numerator and denominator come to you.

STEP 3: Jot down the ratio:

My current HtBR is _____

What prompted me to choose that ratio?

_____

_____

_____

_____

_____

_____

_____

My current HtBR is _____

What prompted me to choose that ratio?

_____

_____

_____

_____

_____

_____

_____

My current HtBR is _____

What prompted me to choose that ratio?

_____

_____

_____

_____

_____

_____

_____

CELEBRATING CHANGE

Pausing and spending a few moments acknowledging your experience and celebrating it has many healing benefits. You can celebrate the experience in any way you choose, but the important thing is to really mean it and feel it. This may be difficult at first, so try imagining that you're celebrating a friend's accomplishments. For example, if you choose to celebrate with a positive statement like "Way to go!" say this to yourself like you would say it to a close friend. Feel the excitement, pride, and celebratory vibe in your body.

What would I like to celebrate today?

How will I celebrate?

_____

_____

_____

_____

_____

_____

_____

How do I feel when I take the time to celebrate a win today?

_____

_____

_____

_____

_____

_____

_____

_____

_____

FREEZE FRAME AWARENESS

Like a snapshot in time, this exercise is designed to build your awareness of feeling your body in positions that compromise your health. Try this once a day to give yourself an opportunity to release tension.

STEP 1: When a moment occurs when you find you're gripping or holding a tense posture, take a pause.

STEP 2: Notice your held muscle tension without self-judgment.

STEP 3: Breathe into the tensed area, and on the exhale, explore how you can release this extra effort (i.e., relax your shoulders to where they normally rest).

STEP 4: Slowly breathe in and out of the area you just released for at least five breaths.

STEP 5: Sit quietly and simply notice how you feel.

Where did you notice tension?

How did it feel to release that tension?

_____

_____

_____

_____

_____

_____

_____

How do you feel when you take the time to do this daily?

_____

_____

_____

_____

_____

_____

_____

_____

BODY-FOCUSED BREATHING

This exercise will enhance your ability to locate tension in your body.
Through conscious use of your breath, you'll become increasingly aware
of how the tension shows up, as well as your ability to release it.

STEP 1: With your eyes closed, scan your body and notice where your body is holding tension.

STEP 2: Inhale into the area of tension and exhale.

STEP 3: Remaining focused on the specific area of tension in your body, repeat Step 2 a few more times (at least five, and upward to as many as you'd like). Notice how your body feels and how your posture may have shifted.

Where did you notice tension?

_____

_____

_____

_____

_____

_____

_____

_____

_____

_____

How did it feel to release that tension?

_____

_____

_____

_____

_____

_____

_____

How do you feel when you take the time to do this daily?

_____

_____

_____

_____

_____

_____

_____

_____

BREATHING SLOWLY

Breathing more slowly builds your capacity to breathe deeply with more ease. As you move out of the habit of shallow breathing, this exercise will help you gradually open your lungs to a fuller capacity so you can breathe deeply.

STEP 1: Begin seated with your eyes closed and notice your breath. Don't try to change your breathing pattern in any way; observe without judgment.

STEP 2: After you've followed your inhalation and exhalation for a few rounds, count the inhale from start to finish. Then count the exhale from start to finish. This will give you a number to work with, such as "three counts in and four counts out."

STEP 3: Now, continue breathing in and out to that same count, and begin to slow your count down. You'll still inhale to that same count of three and exhale to the same count of four, but your count between each number will become longer to slow your breathing down. Complete at least ten rounds of this slowed breathing exercise.

STEP 4: To finish, release the count, breathe as your body naturally does, and spend a few moments noticing how your body feels. This exercise will be tricky at first, but with a bit of practice, you'll get the hang of it.

What did you notice about your breathing at the beginning of this exercise?

_____

_____

_____

_____

_____

_____

_____

_____

How did your body feel by the end of the exercise?

_____

_____

_____

_____

_____

_____

_____

_____

IDENTIFY YOUR BURNOUT METAPHOR

The premise of this practice is to get in touch with the deeper visceral levels of your burnout through the use of metaphor. Once you identify an appropriate metaphor for your burnout in this exercise, you'll use that metaphor in a guided meditation on page 46.

Think about how you would metaphorically describe your burnout by tuning in to your body to feel your visceral experience of burnout. For help, review the examples provided. Then see which metaphor resonates with your experience, or create your own.

- ○ White-knuckling it through life
- ○ Working my way into a corner that I need to get myself out of
- ○ Feeling like I'm getting pulled in different directions at 100 mph
- ○ A drained battery that can no longer hold a charge
- ○ A long, dark tunnel with seemingly no end
- ○ Being on a hamster wheel that self-propels ever faster

Do you identify with any of these metaphors? If so, in what ways?

_____

_____

_____

_____

_____

_____

_____

_____

_____

_____

Create your own burnout metaphor below:

_____

_____

_____

_____

_____

_____

_____

_____

_____

_____

_____

_____

MEDITATION FOR LETTING GO

In this exercise, you'll create a guided meditation using your burnout metaphor (see page 44) that visually undoes your feeling of stuckness so you can learn to let go of stress. I recommend doing this practice daily for at least a week and observing how your body, mind, mood, and energy levels shift.

STEP 1: Begin seated or standing (whatever makes the most sense, given your metaphor) and close your eyes.

STEP 2: Spend a few moments getting grounded within your body. (If it helps, you could say, *I'm aware that I am sitting/standing right now.*)

STEP 3: Then bring your burnout metaphor into your mind's eye and envision yourself experiencing it. As an example, see and feel the tension and terror of "white-knuckling it through life," in both your body and mind.

STEP 4: Now, begin to allow the constraints of the metaphor to loosen as you visualize its release. Continuing with the "white-knuckling" example, imagine the engine slowing down as you release the visceral grip of your burnout experience. You will start to feel lighter; you can breathe more slowly and fully.

STEP 5: To finish the exercise, remain quiet and still. Notice how your internal sense of burnout may have shifted.

How did you feel as you visualized releasing your burnout?

_____

_____

_____

_____

_____

_____

_____

Over the course of a week, how did this exercise affect your body, mind, mood, and energy levels?

_____

_____

_____

_____

_____

_____

_____

HELPFUL AND UNHELPFUL THOUGHTS

As a rule of thumb, beware of unhelpful thoughts that make you feel as if you're defeated, constricted, or stuck in a rut. Helpful thoughts, on the other hand, feel expansive and nurture you through kindness; they reinforce self-trust in your growth potential. Through this process of changing your mind to create thought patterns that lift you out of burnout and facilitate long-term wellness, you will ask yourself, *Is this a helpful thought?*

Identify a recent unhelpful thought. What was it?

_____

_____

_____

_____

How did this unhelpful thought make you feel, in both your mind and body?

_____

_____

_____

_____

_____

_____

_____

Identify a recent helpful thought. What was it?

_____

_____

_____

_____

_____

_____

How did this helpful thought make you feel, in both your mind and body?

_____

_____

_____

_____

_____

_____

_____

I DON'T HAVE ENOUGH...

This exercise will help you increase your awareness of how thoughts and beliefs of scarcity show up for you, while building a willingness to think about yourself in a new way.

Sit quietly and take a few breaths to ground yourself. Then, fill in the blank to finish this sentence:

"I don't have enough _____."

Repeat the statement. How does this thought feel in your body?

_____

_____

_____

_____

_____

_____

_____

_____

_____

_____

_____

_____

Next, follow a new train of thought: *What if I'm enough right now? What if I know I'm doing the best I can with the tools and information I have?* How does it feel in your body to tell yourself that you are enough?

How do you feel after repeating this exercise daily for a week?

IDENTIFY YOUR MIND TRAPS

Mind traps keep you thinking in the same ways, coming to the same conclusions, and reliving the same problems. By reviewing the following mind traps, you'll start to liberate yourself from old patterns and unhelpful ways of thinking.

MIND READER: Believing you know what someone else is thinking without checking in with them.

CATASTROPHIZING: This is when you expect the worst to happen, or you believe when something bad does happen, it's the worst thing ever.

LABELING: This is a way of name-calling that either discounts yourself or another person, such as calling yourself or someone else a "loser."

PERFECTIONISM: Believing the lie that there's one perfect way to do something.

DISCOUNTING AND FILTERING: This happens when you pay attention to negative events and/or discount positive experiences, by thinking that they're untrue or don't count.

ALL OR NOTHING: These thoughts frequently include absolutes (like "never" or "always") and extreme rules or categories, making something either "all good" or "all bad."

EMOTIONAL REASONING: This happens when you base your judgments, decisions, and conclusions exclusively on your feelings (especially when you're stressed) and believe that if you feel a certain way then it must be true.

Which of these mind traps do you think apply to you?

_____

_____

_____

_____

_____

_____

_____

Can you identify a way one of these mind traps recently played out in your interactions with yourself or other people?

_____

_____

_____

_____

_____

_____

_____

SPIRALING UP!

Sometimes it can feel all too easy to get caught in the downward spiral of distressing thoughts (catastrophizing), which leads you into further despair and becoming stuck in stress mode. But what if there's another way? What if you can teach your mind and body to "spiral up" with a succession of helpful thoughts that lead to joy and endless possibility? This teaches you how to do just that.

STEP 1: Create a "what if" statement for something you worry about often:
(Example: What if I bomb my presentation at work and get fired?)

_____

_____

_____

STEP 2: Recreate that "what if" statement into a better scenario:
(Example: What if I ace the presentation at work and get a promotion?)

_____

_____

_____

_____

_____

_____

STEP 3: Stand up, feel solid and grounded with your feet about hip-width apart and planted firmly on the ground. Feel the entire length of your body extend from the floor all the way up through the top of your head. Now, say the "what if" statement from step 1 (out loud or to yourself). Notice how this thought feels in your body. Then, switch to the "what if" statement from step 2 and notice how this changes your body's response.

STEP 4: Continue to repeat this second "what if" statement again and again, adding even better scenarios as you reach for the best-case scenario you could imagine.

STEP 5: As you spiral up, get your body into the mix by jumping up and down or waving your arms in the air. Really get into it as you celebrate your life without limitations. Continue spiraling up for one to four minutes.

STEP 6: When you're done, stand quietly, close your eyes, and notice the changes in your mind, mood, and body.

How did your body feel when you said both statements?

_____

_____

_____

_____

_____

_____

_____

_____

_____

_____

_____

_____

What even better scenarios were you able to imagine?

Over the course of a week, how did this exercise affect your body, mind, mood, and energy levels?

REWIRE YOUR BRAIN

As you build awareness of your habitual thoughts, you can make the conscious choice to eliminate unhelpful thoughts by replacing them with helpful ones. When practiced consistently, this exercise will rewire your brain with helpful thought patterns that support your well-being.

When you become aware that you're engaged in a mind trap or are thinking an unhelpful thought, stop and work through this exercise.

What is the unhelpful thought?

_____

_____

_____

_____

_____

_____

Label the statement for what it is, e.g. *That's an unhelpful thought*, or *That's a false belief*. Write your label here:

_____

_____

_____

_____

_____

Do a simple, general reframe of your thought, e.g. *From now on, I choose only helpful thoughts that support my well-being*. Write your reframe here:

Write a helpful thought that's specific to your situation, e.g. *I just called myself an idiot. That's untrue, I'm actually really smart*. Write your helpful thought here:

NOTICING "SHOULD"

This exercise teaches you to become aware of the social pervasiveness of the use of "should." In the exercises that follow this one, you'll practice effective reframes that will over time become automatic thoughts in place of unhelpful "should" thoughts.

Start to notice the pervasive use of "should" statements that you and other people make throughout your day. Write a few of them down here:

_____

_____

_____

_____

_____

_____

_____

_____

_____

_____

_____

_____

_____

Also notice the emotions you link to these statements when you hear them (i.e., guilt, shame, regret). What are some of these emotions?

_____

_____

_____

_____

If you find it helpful, begin to keep a tally below, marking off each time you say the word "should."

_____

Start a second tally for how often you hear it being used by someone else.

_____

Do this without judgment or condemnation for at least two days, while remaining curious as you take stock of this social norm. Note how it affects your mood.

_____

_____

_____

_____

_____

_____

PHASING "SHOULD" OUT OF YOUR LIFE

You're now at the phase of consciously removing "should" from your habitual way of thinking and speaking—and you may be surprised at how easy this process becomes once you've become so aware.

Begin to reframe your "should" statements. This can be done in two main ways:

(1) Replace "should" with "could," or

(2) Replace "should" with something like *It would likely benefit me if I . . .*

An example of optional reframes for *I should go to the gym* include:

(1) *I could go to the gym*, or

(2) *It would likely benefit me if I go to the gym*.

As you remain consistent with this reframe practice, you'll begin to notice when you're about to say "should" right before it happens. At this point, change it to "could" or another affirming phrase. Record some of the "should" statements you noticed along with the reframes you used below.

(1) Should statement:

_____

(2) Could reframe:

_____

(3) Other reframe:

_____

(1) Should statement:

_____

(2) Could reframe:

_____

(3) Other reframe:

_____

(1) Should statement:

_____

(2) Could reframe:

_____

(3) Other reframe:

_____

(1) Should statement:

_____

(2) Could reframe:

_____

(3) Other reframe:

_____

MINDFUL SLOW-MO

This is one of my favorite ways to relish the present moment at a slowed pace. Through your focused attention on the slow muscle movement of your body, you can retrain your mind to quiet down and stop "overthinking."

STEP 1: While standing with your eyes open, begin to move and stretch your body in any way that feels good. Let your body intuitively take the lead. There's nothing to think about—just move and feel into the sensations of your stretched muscles.

STEP 2: When you're ready, begin to slow the movement down, mindfully observing both the physical movement and the sensations of your body in motion as it moves at a slower and slower pace.

STEP 3: Move as slowly as you can for as long as you want. If your awareness drifts, simply return your focus to your body's movement.

STEP 4: Next, try moving only one section of your body (such as your forearm through to your hand). While moving this area slowly, observe with curiosity.

STEP 5: To finish, slow your body into stillness, close your eyes, and simply notice how your mind, mood, and body have responded to this exercise.

How did this experience shift me internally?

In what ways can I be more myself when I slow down?

What are some other ways that I can inspire myself to become still?

How can I bring what I'm learning here into my everyday life?

EMOTION IDENTIFICATION

This exercise is designed to help you identify your emotions and gain a deeper understanding of your current relationship with emotions.

Review the partial list of human emotions below and write down the emotions that correspond to the following questions. If you don't see an emotion on the list, add your own. Keep this list as a visual guide and refer back to it as you learn to identify, allow, explore, feel, and release your emotions.

Acceptance	Care	Exhilaration
Affection	Cheer	Expectancy
Aggravation	Compassion	Fear
Aggression	Confidence	Fondness
Agitation	Confusion	Forgiveness
Alarm	Contempt	Fury
Amazement	Curiosity	Gloom
Ambivalence	Cynicism	Gratitude
Amusement	Danger	Grief
Anger	Delight	Grouchiness
Annoyance	Depression	Guilt
Anxiety	Desire	Happiness
Apathy	Detachment	Hatred
Astonishment	Disappointment	Hesitancy
Attachment	Disgust	Hope
Attraction	Doubt	Horror
Belonging	Ecstasy	Hostility
Bitterness	Embarrassment	Humiliation
Blame	Empathy	Hunger
Bliss	Envy	Insecurity
Boredom	Euphoria	Interest
Buoyancy	Excitement	Intimidation

Irritation	Pleasure	Suffering
Jealousy	Pride	Surprise
Joy	Protection	Suspicion
Judgment	Rage	Sympathy
Loneliness	Regret	Tenderness
Love	Remorse	Terror
Nervousness	Resentment	Uncertainty
Optimism	Revulsion	Vigilance
Overwhelm	Sadness	Vulnerability
Panic	Shame	Worry
Paranoia	Shyness	Zeal
Passion	Skepticism	

Which emotions were more allowed in your family?

_____

_____

_____

_____

_____

Which emotions are most allowed in the workplace?

_____

_____

_____

_____

_____

Which emotions do you allow yourself to openly feel in private?

Which emotions do you allow yourself to openly feel in public?

Which emotions are lying just under the surface that you're trying not to feel?

_____

_____

_____

_____

_____

_____

_____

Which emotions do you want to feel, but they lie dormant under burnout?

_____

_____

_____

_____

_____

_____

_____

RELEASING EMOTIONS

Since being overly identified with an emotion or avoiding it at all costs constricts your capacity to healthfully process your emotions, you'll now practice releasing your mind's need to take control for 90 seconds and learn how to let your body do what's needed to feel the emotion and then let it go.

STEP 1: Notice your current emotional state and set a timer for 90 seconds.

STEP 2: Label your current and predominant emotion (refer to the emotions list on page 68 for help).

STEP 3: Close your eyes and observe how the emotion is showing up as sensations in your body.

STEP 4: Breathe in and out of those sensations to create space between you and the emotion (remember the emotion is not you).

STEP 5: Each time you notice your mind wandering to a story about the emotion, return awareness to your breath and body.

STEP 6: Without force or expectation, allow the emotion to shift and move at will.

STEP 7: When the 90 seconds are up, spend a few moments in silent reflection.

Describe your emotional state when you began the exercise:

_____

_____

_____

_____

_____

_____

_____

Describe how your emotions changed over the course of the exercise:

_____

_____

_____

_____

_____

_____

_____

_____

PROCESSING FEAR

Through this mantra-based exploratory practice, you will train your mind to work with your body in order to locate fear within you. You'll then consciously give it permission to be released.

STEP 1: Say each of the following mantras to yourself and follow your own instructions. Between each mantra, pause and mindfully notice the response of your mind and body. Remain curious and observant.

1. Through my mind, I allow fear to arise in my body.

2. Through my mind, I recognize the sensations in my body and label them as "fear."

3. Through my body, I breathe in and out of the fear spaces in my body.

4. Through my mind and body, I observe with curiosity how the breath creates space and shifts the presentation of fear in my body.

5. Through my mind, I reinforce the truth that in this very moment I am safe.

6. Through my mind, while remaining very grounded in my body, I allow the release of fear.

STEP 2: Then say:

1. Thank you, fear, for all the ways you have protected me.

2. I forgive you, fear, for all the ways you have helped me limit myself.

3. I no longer need you, fear, so I lovingly release you.

4. From now on, I acknowledge fear when it arises, and I'm open to love.

What responses did you notice in your body and mind during this exercise?

How did you feel by the end of the exercise?

AWARENESS MEDITATION

This exercise teaches you how to gain perspective about your emotions by reinforcing the message within your body and mind that each emotion is part of your human experience, yet it's not who you are. Through this simple awareness meditation, you can be with any emotion without becoming either fully identified with it or trying to avoid it.

STEP 1: Begin seated with your eyes closed and notice your emotional state.

STEP 2: As you become aware of what you're feeling, say to yourself, *I'm aware that I'm feeling this way.*

STEP 3: After a few moments, add, *I'm aware that I'm aware that I'm feeling this way.*

STEP 4: Be with this new and expanded experience for a few more moments.

STEP 5: Begin to notice that from this vantage point you are an active yet neutral observer of your own experience, who recognizes the emotion is not you.

STEP 6: Be with this experience for as long as you'd like, and when you're ready, open your eyes and return to your day.

What was your emotional state at the beginning of this meditation?

What did it feel like to observe your emotional state with more distance?

PRACTICE BREATHING WELL

By choosing to practice a breathing style with an extended exhale, you're consciously turning on your body's relaxation response and undoing the habit of shallow and held breath. The more you practice, the more in tune you will become to your breath.

STEP 1: Wherever you are, begin to notice your breath. Are you holding your breath, are you breathing in your upper chest and throat, or are you breathing deeper into your lungs? Without judgment, simply notice.

STEP 2: Consciously and slowly breathe out of your nose (you're starting the breath cycle with an exhale).

STEP 3: Breathe in and through your nose for a count of three.

STEP 4: Breathe out and through your nose for a count of five.

STEP 5: Continue with this breathing pattern.

STEP 6: As you get acquainted with this breathing pattern, notice if you can extend your breath even further down into your lungs for a deeper breath.

STEP 7: To finish, release focus from your breath. Remain quiet and notice the after-effects in your mind, emotions, and physical body.

What did you notice about your breath at the beginning of this exercise?

_____

_____

_____

_____

_____

_____

_____

_____

What effects did this exercise have on your mind, emotions, and body?

_____

_____

_____

_____

_____

_____

_____

_____

UPLEVEL YOUR MOOD

This practice enables acknowledgment, appreciation, and release of depleting emotions, while authentically transitioning to a preferred feeling.

STEP 1: Notice when a depleting emotion arises (i.e., fear, judgment, doubt, worry).

STEP 2: Get curious and allow it to be there.

STEP 3: Choose gratitude for the depleting emotion, knowing it has served to protect you in the past and has risen to the surface of your consciousness to now be released.

STEP 4: Decide how you want to feel in this moment and choose that healing emotion.

What depleting emotion were you experiencing?

_____

_____

_____

_____

_____

_____

_____

_____

_____

How did it feel to release and replace that emotion?

_____

_____

_____

_____

_____

_____

_____

_____

How did this exercise affect your emotions throughout the rest of your day?

_____

_____

_____

_____

_____

_____

_____

_____

_____

REWORKING BUSYNESS

Busyness is a habit that keeps you going at a pace, and in a manner, that's not sustainable, reduces overall productivity, and is mentally exhausting. You can have a full schedule without the felt sense of being busy; it just takes some rewiring of your mind and body to shift your mindset from "busyness equals effectiveness" to one that offers a calmer solution. This exercise helps create this new perspective, as you slow your nervous system down in the face of intensity.

STEP 1: Sit quietly with your eyes closed for one minute and watch your thoughts. Don't try to halt them in any way. Simply observe with nonjudgment.

STEP 2: Stand up and begin to move your body in a way that matches the pace and intensity of your thoughts. Thrash your arms and body around as much as you can with your eyes open. Do this for a full minute, making your body as busy as you possibly can.

STEP 3: Then stop! Close your eyes with your feet placed firmly on the ground, standing tall, with one hand on your heart and one hand on your belly. Be still and breathe until your heart rate returns to resting state.

STEP 4: Self-reflect on your experience from intense action (busyness) into stillness.

Consider what would happen if all of the busyness stopped and I hit the pause button in the midst of a workday frenzy. What would I see?

_____

_____

_____

_____

_____

_____

_____

What is actually going on?

_____

_____

_____

_____

_____

_____

_____

_____

What could I get rid of?

What do I want to keep?

ENCOURAGING SILLINESS

Gathering from informal surveys of my workshop participants, it's near unanimous that people love to be silly. Yet most adults stop allowing themselves to be silly. This exercise will remind you how fun it is to be silly and encourage you to be sillier more often, which in and of itself is a great stress reliever! After this exercise, you'll not only feel freer, but you'll also reinforce to your body and mind that your values don't necessarily align with the constraints of prescribed social values. You can be you and be an adult.

STEP 1: Do the Mindful Slow-Mo exercise on page 64 through step 4.

STEP 2: Then, instead of "slow your body into stillness" in step 5, move your body into silliness.

STEP 3: Move in as many bizarre and unexpected ways as you can come up with. Allow your mind and body to work in tandem as you move in sillier and sillier ways.

STEP 4: Allow yourself to laugh, make weird noises and funny faces, smile, and enjoy.

STEP 5: To finish, stand with your eyes closed and feel into the resonance of this experience.

How did you feel after doing this exercise?

_____

_____

_____

_____

_____

_____

_____

What are some ways you could incorporate more silliness into your everyday life?

_____

_____

_____

_____

_____

_____

_____

_____

GETTING CLEAR ON YOUR "WHY"

By working through this exercise, you'll be able to clarify and prioritize your heartfelt personal values that support your meaningful life.

STEP 1: Thoughtfully review the list of personal values on the opposite page. Be mindful to not choose values just because they sound good or you think you should value them—to be your "why" they must resonate with you.

STEP 2: Circle the values that are important to you right now (or add ones not already listed in the blank spaces).

STEP 3: Highlight or check off ten values that are very important to you.

STEP 4: Placing a number next to your top values, rank these ten from most to least important, with number one being the MOST important to you.

Acceptance	Ethical	Leadership	Risk
Accountability	Expressive	Logic	Satisfaction
Accuracy	Fairness	Love	Security
Achievement	Family	Loyalty	Sensitivity
Adaptability	Famous	Mastery	Simplicity
Assertiveness	Focus	Maturity	Sincerity
Attentiveness	Freedom	Meaning	Solitude
Balance	Friendship	Moderation	Spirituality
Beauty	Fun	Motivation	Spontaneous
Boldness	Generosity	Openness	Stability
Calm	Genuineness	Optimism	Teamwork
Capable	Grace	Organization	Thoughtful
Challenge	Gratitude	Originality	Timeliness
Charity	Growth	Passion	Traditional
Clarity	Harmony	Patience	Transparency
Clever	Health	Performance	Trust
Comfort	Honesty	Persistence	Uniqueness
Commitment	Honor	Playfulness	Vitality
Communication	Imagination	Poise	Wealth
Community	Independence	Potential	Winning
Compassion	Individuality	Productivity	Wisdom
Connection	Innovation	Professionalism	Wonder
Consistency	Insightful	Prosperity	Others:
Creativity	Integrity	Purpose	
Curiosity	Intelligence	Quality	
Dedication	Intimacy	Realistic	
Dignity	Joy	Recognition	
Discipline	Justice	Recreation	
Drive	Kindness	Reflective	
Efficiency	Knowledge	Respect	
Empathy	Lawful	Responsibility	

What came up for you during this exercise? Were there any surprises?

In what ways are you already aligned with your values?

What things that don't align with your values can you begin to let go of?

_____

_____

_____

_____

_____

_____

_____

What can you shift or change in your day that will align yourself more with your values?

_____

_____

_____

_____

_____

_____

_____

ESSENCE OF YOUR VALUES

~~~~~~~~~~~~~~~~~~~~~~~~~~~~~~

This meditation will help you tune in to your wellspring of energy and inner guidance by sensing into your chosen personal values that give your mind and body a deeper sense of safety, meaning, and purpose.

STEP 1: Choose a personal value from the list on page 89.

STEP 2: Closing your eyes, begin to quiet down and focus on your breath. Feel yourself present and aware.

STEP 3: Begin to cultivate the lived experience of your chosen value in your body. Imagine how it would feel if you were living it right now and deepen your awareness inward. (If it helps, recall a specific memory of a time you were living by this personal value.)

STEP 4: Sense into the energetic response of your body. Be with it and explore it with curiosity.

STEP 5: When complete, sit for a few moments in quiet reflection.

Which value did you choose?

_____

_____

_____

_____

_____

_____

_____

_____

How did you feel when you imagined living by this value?

_____

_____

_____

_____

_____

_____

What are some ways you could live by this value in your everyday life?

_____

_____

_____

_____

_____

_____

_____

BEING MINDFUL ABOUT MEDIA

This exercise is designed to help you get clear on your daily media intake so you can best choose your relationship with media going forward.

STEP 1: Keep a log of your digital media use for three days.

STEP 2: Along with the platform type, make note of profiles/accounts that align with your values and uplift and inspire. Also make note of those that have the opposite effect.

STEP 3: At the end of the three days, review the log and decide what you want to keep and what you want to release.

STEP 4: Unfollow all accounts that hinder your well-being.

What platform did I use?	How long did I use it?	What aligned with my values or inspired me?	What did not align with my values or depleted me?

What platform did I use?	How long did I use it?	What aligned with my values or inspired me?	What did not align with my values or depleted me?

What platform did I use?	How long did I use it?	What aligned with my values or inspired me?	What did not align with my values or depleted me?

SETTING BOUNDARIES

Here, you'll devise and execute a plan to set an important boundary in your life that will support a burnout-free lifestyle. Answer the following prompts to complete your action plan.

What is something or someone that you would benefit from setting a boundary with?

_____

_____

_____

_____

_____

_____

Which personal values support this choice?

_____

_____

_____

_____

_____

_____

_____

66

What will you do or say to set this boundary?

_____

_____

_____

_____

_____

_____

_____

_____

_____

When and where will you do it?

_____

_____

_____

_____

_____

_____

_____

_____

_____

_____

What uncomfortable emotions do you anticipate will come up for you?

What may be some good emotions that will arise as a result?

What are some avoidant or discouraging thoughts you may have?

_____
_____
_____
_____
_____
_____
_____

How will you manage your emotions and thoughts?

_____
_____
_____
_____
_____
_____
_____

GUIDED INTO WHOLENESS

This practice connects you to all the aspects of yourself in present moment awareness to deepen your sense of wholeness.

STEP 1: Sit quietly with your eyes closed and begin to notice your physical body. Through your internal awareness, scan your whole body and breathe into the tension areas and then release. Ease your posture into a comfortable yet upright position. Be with this experience for about one minute.

STEP 2: Become aware of your emotional state and sense into it within your body. Remain present as the observer of your emotions and return your focus to these sensations in your body whenever your mind wanders. Be with this experience for about one minute.

STEP 3: Now notice your mind and continue to use it as an awareness tool to remain present within your being. When you become aware of a thought taking you into the past or future, return your focus to what's happening now. Be with this experience for about one minute.

STEP 4: Going deeper into your body, choose a personal value (see page 89) and be with the energy of your heartfelt principle. If helpful, recall a time when you were living this value. Be with this experience for about one minute.

STEP 5: While in this heartfelt state, notice your thoughts, emotions, and physical body. Be with all of it and stay with this whole presence for one to two minutes.

STEP 6: To finish, say to yourself, *I am whole, I am well.* Then spend a few moments in quiet reflection of your practice.

What did you notice about your body, emotions, and mind during this exercise?

How did you feel after you completed this practice?

"I CHOOSE ME" MANTRA MEDITATION

In a society that has taught you to place everyone else's needs before your own, this mantra meditation rewires your body and mind to accept and embrace a new paradigm of self-care.

STEP 1: Be quiet with yourself, ground into your body, and become aware of all of you.

STEP 2: With your eyes closed or open, begin to repeat the mantra, *I choose me.*

STEP 3: Notice any thoughts and emotions that arise.

STEP 4: Return your focus to your mantra (each return is a "thought reframe").

STEP 5: As you continue to repeat this mantra, cultivate the inner tone of your self-care values.

STEP 6: Keep going and be with this experience.

STEP 7: To finish, end the mantra and sit with your experience in self-reflection.

What thoughts and emotions came up for you during this exercise?

How did you feel after this exercise?

THEN AND NOW

Through these writing prompts, this exercise is designed for self-reflection and acknowledgment of your progress thus far.

Since the first day I engaged with this journal, how has my relationship with my body, emotions, thoughts, and energy changed?

Since the first day I engaged with this journal, how has my relationship with my outer world changed?

Continuing Wellness Plan

Now that you've begun the work of healing from burnout, it's time to make a plan to create sustained wellness in your life. In the following pages, you'll map out a daily practice that will support your ongoing healing and evolving sense of well-being. Remember, your plan can change as you heal and evolve—there are multiple pages to write out new plans as you need them.

YOUR CONTINUING WELLNESS PLAN

This exercise helps to create a daily set of awareness activities to sustain a holistic sense of who you are, even in the midst of a busy workday. Review and consider all of the exercises you have practiced in this journal so far and complete the following prompts.

What exercise(s) will I do before work each day?

_____

_____

_____

_____

What exercise(s) will I do to make sure I have at least three mini-breaks during each workday?

_____

_____

_____

_____

Do I need to set an alert on my phone as a reminder to do them? ☐ Yes   ☐ No

What after-work exercise(s) will I do to help me decompress so I can get quality sleep?

_____

_____

_____

_____

What external obstacles may get in the way of this plan? How can I overcome them?

_____

_____

_____

_____

_____

What internal obstacles may get in the way of this plan? How can I overcome them?

_____

_____

_____

_____

_____

What personal values align with my reason to stick with this daily practice?

_____

_____

_____

_____

_____

The date I will start this plan is: _____

And I hold myself accountable now [initials] _____

What exercise(s) will I do before work each day?

_____

_____

_____

_____

_____

What exercise(s) will I do to make sure I have at least three mini-breaks during each workday?

_____

_____

_____

_____

_____

Do I need to set an alert on my phone as a reminder to do them? ☐ Yes   ☐ No

What after-work exercise(s) will I do to help me decompress so I can get quality sleep?

_____

_____

_____

_____

_____

What external obstacles may get in the way of this plan? How can I overcome them?

_____

_____

_____

_____

_____

What internal obstacles may get in the way of this plan? How can I overcome them?

_____

_____

_____

_____

_____

What personal values align with my reason to stick with this daily practice?

_____

_____

_____

_____

_____

The date I will start this plan is: _____

And I hold myself accountable now [initials] _____

What exercise(s) will I do before work each day?

_____

_____

_____

_____

What exercise(s) will I do to make sure I have at least three mini-breaks during each workday?

_____

_____

_____

_____

Do I need to set an alert on my phone as a reminder to do them? ☐ Yes   ☐ No

What after-work exercise(s) will I do to help me decompress so I can get quality sleep?

_____

_____

_____

_____

_____

What external obstacles may get in the way of this plan? How can I overcome them?

_____

_____

_____

_____

_____

What internal obstacles may get in the way of this plan? How can I overcome them?

_____

_____

_____

_____

What personal values align with my reason to stick with this daily practice?

_____

_____

_____

_____

The date I will start this plan is: _____

And I hold myself accountable now [initials] _____

What exercise(s) will I do before work each day?

_____

_____

_____

_____

_____

What exercise(s) will I do to make sure I have at least three mini-breaks during each workday?

_____

_____

_____

_____

_____

Do I need to set an alert on my phone as a reminder to do them? ☐ Yes ☐ No

What after-work exercise(s) will I do to help me decompress so I can get quality sleep?

_____

_____

_____

_____

_____

_____

What external obstacles may get in the way of this plan? How can I overcome them?

_____

_____

_____

_____

_____

What internal obstacles may get in the way of this plan? How can I overcome them?

_____

_____

_____

_____

_____

What personal values align with my reason to stick with this daily practice?

_____

_____

_____

_____

_____

The date I will start this plan is: _____

And I hold myself accountable now [initials] _____

What exercise(s) will I do before work each day?

_____

_____

_____

_____

_____

What exercise(s) will I do to make sure I have at least three mini-breaks during each workday?

_____

_____

_____

_____

_____

Do I need to set an alert on my phone as a reminder to do them? ☐ Yes   ☐ No

What after-work exercise(s) will I do to help me decompress so I can get quality sleep?

_____

_____

_____

_____

_____

What external obstacles may get in the way of this plan? How can I overcome them?

_____

_____

_____

_____

_____

What internal obstacles may get in the way of this plan? How can I overcome them?

_____

_____

_____

_____

_____

What personal values align with my reason to stick with this daily practice?

_____

_____

_____

_____

_____

The date I will start this plan is: _____

And I hold myself accountable now [initials]   _____

What exercise(s) will I do before work each day?

_____

_____

_____

_____

_____

What exercise(s) will I do to make sure I have at least three mini-breaks during each workday?

_____

_____

_____

_____

_____

Do I need to set an alert on my phone as a reminder to do them? ☐ Yes ☐ No

What after-work exercise(s) will I do to help me decompress so I can get quality sleep?

_____

_____

_____

_____

_____

What external obstacles may get in the way of this plan? How can I overcome them?

_____

_____

_____

_____

_____

What internal obstacles may get in the way of this plan? How can I overcome them?

_____

_____

_____

_____

_____

What personal values align with my reason to stick with this daily practice?

_____

_____

_____

_____

_____

The date I will start this plan is: _____

And I hold myself accountable now [initials] _____

What exercise(s) will I do before work each day?

_____

_____

_____

_____

_____

What exercise(s) will I do to make sure I have at least three mini-breaks during each workday?

_____

_____

_____

_____

_____

Do I need to set an alert on my phone as a reminder to do them? ☐ Yes   ☐ No

What after-work exercise(s) will I do to help me decompress so I can get quality sleep?

_____

_____

_____

_____

_____

_____

What external obstacles may get in the way of this plan? How can I overcome them?

_____

_____

_____

_____

_____

What internal obstacles may get in the way of this plan? How can I overcome them?

_____

_____

_____

_____

_____

What personal values align with my reason to stick with this daily practice?

_____

_____

_____

_____

_____

The date I will start this plan is: _____

And I hold myself accountable now [initials] _____

What exercise(s) will I do before work each day?

_____

_____

_____

_____

What exercise(s) will I do to make sure I have at least three mini-breaks during each workday?

_____

_____

_____

_____

Do I need to set an alert on my phone as a reminder to do them? ☐ Yes ☐ No

What after-work exercise(s) will I do to help me decompress so I can get quality sleep?

_____

_____

_____

_____

_____

What external obstacles may get in the way of this plan? How can I overcome them?

_____

_____

_____

_____

_____

What internal obstacles may get in the way of this plan? How can I overcome them?

_____

_____

_____

_____

_____

What personal values align with my reason to stick with this daily practice?

_____

_____

_____

_____

_____

The date I will start this plan is: _____

And I hold myself accountable now [initials] _____

What exercise(s) will I do before work each day?

_____

_____

_____

_____

_____

What exercise(s) will I do to make sure I have at least three mini-breaks during each workday?

_____

_____

_____

_____

_____

Do I need to set an alert on my phone as a reminder to do them? ☐ Yes ☐ No

What after-work exercise(s) will I do to help me decompress so I can get quality sleep?

_____

_____

_____

_____

_____

_____

What external obstacles may get in the way of this plan? How can I overcome them?

_____

_____

_____

_____

_____

What internal obstacles may get in the way of this plan? How can I overcome them?

_____

_____

_____

_____

_____

What personal values align with my reason to stick with this daily practice?

_____

_____

_____

_____

_____

The date I will start this plan is: _____

And I hold myself accountable now [initials] _____

What exercise(s) will I do before work each day?

_____

_____

_____

_____

_____

What exercise(s) will I do to make sure I have at least three mini-breaks during each workday?

_____

_____

_____

_____

_____

Do I need to set an alert on my phone as a reminder to do them? ☐ Yes   ☐ No

What after-work exercise(s) will I do to help me decompress so I can get quality sleep?

_____

_____

_____

_____

_____

_____

What external obstacles may get in the way of this plan? How can I overcome them?

_____

_____

_____

_____

_____

What internal obstacles may get in the way of this plan? How can I overcome them?

_____

_____

_____

_____

_____

What personal values align with my reason to stick with this daily practice?

_____

_____

_____

_____

_____

The date I will start this plan is: _____

And I hold myself accountable now [initials] _____

What exercise(s) will I do before work each day?

_____

_____

_____

_____

_____

What exercise(s) will I do to make sure I have at least three mini-breaks during each workday?

_____

_____

_____

_____

_____

Do I need to set an alert on my phone as a reminder to do them? ☐ Yes   ☐ No

What after-work exercise(s) will I do to help me decompress so I can get quality sleep?

_____

_____

_____

_____

_____

What external obstacles may get in the way of this plan? How can I overcome them?

_____

_____

_____

_____

_____

What internal obstacles may get in the way of this plan? How can I overcome them?

_____

_____

_____

_____

_____

What personal values align with my reason to stick with this daily practice?

_____

_____

_____

_____

_____

The date I will start this plan is: _____

And I hold myself accountable now [initials] _____

What exercise(s) will I do before work each day?

_____

_____

_____

_____

_____

What exercise(s) will I do to make sure I have at least three mini-breaks during each workday?

_____

_____

_____

_____

Do I need to set an alert on my phone as a reminder to do them? ☐ Yes   ☐ No

What after-work exercise(s) will I do to help me decompress so I can get quality sleep?

_____

_____

_____

_____

_____

What external obstacles may get in the way of this plan? How can I overcome them?

_____

_____

_____

_____

_____

What internal obstacles may get in the way of this plan? How can I overcome them?

_____

_____

_____

_____

_____

What personal values align with my reason to stick with this daily practice?

_____

_____

_____

_____

_____

The date I will start this plan is: _____

And I hold myself accountable now [initials] _____

Visualizing
Future Wellness

In this final section, explore the visceral experience of imagining stepping into your future self. Even if you feel the remnants of burnout, allow this whole-being practice to be your reminder of what's possible—as your inner wisdom guides your healing.

VISUALIZING FUTURE WELLNESS

The power of visualization is taken to the next level in this exercise as you ground into your body and step into your new life of ever-expanding optimal wellness and possibility.

Begin by thinking about who you are without stress, then answer the following questions.

How does my body feel?

_____

_____

_____

What kind of thoughts do I have?

_____

_____

_____

What are the predominant emotions that arise?

_____

_____

_____

How do they align with my heartfelt principles?

_____

_____

_____

Now, imagine a situation where you could be experiencing this in real life. While seated with your eyes closed, picture yourself putting on a virtual-reality headset that allows you to see yourself in first person in the dream situation of your choice. Spend some time exploring your experience in this environment. When feeling ready, remove your virtual headset by opening your eyes. Self-reflect and answer the following questions:

What did you see? How did you move?

_____

_____

_____

How did your body feel?

_____

_____

What were you thinking about?

_____

_____

_____

What was your emotional state?

_____

_____

What was the experience like as you aligned with your values?

_____

_____

_____

Begin by thinking about who you are without stress, then answer the following questions.

How does my body feel?

_____

_____

_____

_____

What kind of thoughts do I have?

_____

_____

_____

_____

What are the predominant emotions that arise?

_____

_____

_____

_____

How do they align with my heartfelt principles?

_____

_____

_____

_____

Now, imagine a situation where you could be experiencing this in real life. While seated with your eyes closed, picture yourself putting on a virtual-reality headset that allows you to see yourself in first person in the dream situation of your choice. Spend some time exploring your experience in this environment. When feeling ready, remove your virtual headset by opening your eyes. Self-reflect and answer the following questions:

What did you see? How did you move?

_____

_____

_____

How did your body feel?

_____

_____

What were you thinking about?

_____

_____

_____

What was your emotional state?

_____

_____

What was the experience like as you aligned with your values?

_____

_____

_____

Begin by thinking about who you are without stress, then answer the following questions.

How does my body feel?

_____

_____

_____

_____

What kind of thoughts do I have?

_____

_____

_____

_____

What are the predominant emotions that arise?

_____

_____

_____

_____

How do they align with my heartfelt principles?

_____

_____

_____

_____

Now, imagine a situation where you could be experiencing this in real life. While seated with your eyes closed, picture yourself putting on a virtual-reality headset that allows you to see yourself in first person in the dream situation of your choice. Spend some time exploring your experience in this environment. When feeling ready, remove your virtual headset by opening your eyes. Self-reflect and answer the following questions:

What did you see? How did you move?

_____

_____

_____

How did your body feel?

_____

_____

What were you thinking about?

_____

_____

_____

What was your emotional state?

_____

_____

What was the experience like as you aligned with your values?

_____

_____

_____

Begin by thinking about who you are without stress, then answer the following questions.

How does my body feel?

_____

_____

_____

_____

What kind of thoughts do I have?

_____

_____

_____

_____

What are the predominant emotions that arise?

_____

_____

_____

_____

How do they align with my heartfelt principles?

_____

_____

_____

_____

Now, imagine a situation where you could be experiencing this in real life. While seated with your eyes closed, picture yourself putting on a virtual-reality headset that allows you to see yourself in first person in the dream situation of your choice. Spend some time exploring your experience in this environment. When feeling ready, remove your virtual headset by opening your eyes. Self-reflect and answer the following questions:

What did you see? How did you move?

_____

_____

_____

How did your body feel?

_____

_____

What were you thinking about?

_____

_____

_____

What was your emotional state?

_____

_____

What was the experience like as you aligned with your values?

_____

_____

_____

Begin by thinking about who you are without stress, then answer the following questions.

How does my body feel?

_____

_____

_____

_____

What kind of thoughts do I have?

_____

_____

_____

_____

What are the predominant emotions that arise?

_____

_____

_____

_____

How do they align with my heartfelt principles?

_____

_____

_____

_____

Now, imagine a situation where you could be experiencing this in real life. While seated with your eyes closed, picture yourself putting on a virtual-reality headset that allows you to see yourself in first person in the dream situation of your choice. Spend some time exploring your experience in this environment. When feeling ready, remove your virtual headset by opening your eyes. Self-reflect and answer the following questions:

What did you see? How did you move?

_____

_____

_____

How did your body feel?

_____

_____

What were you thinking about?

_____

_____

_____

What was your emotional state?

_____

_____

What was the experience like as you aligned with your values?

_____

_____

_____

Begin by thinking about who you are without stress, then answer the following questions.

How does my body feel?

_____

_____

_____

_____

What kind of thoughts do I have?

_____

_____

_____

_____

What are the predominant emotions that arise?

_____

_____

_____

_____

How do they align with my heartfelt principles?

_____

_____

_____

_____

Now, imagine a situation where you could be experiencing this in real life. While seated with your eyes closed, picture yourself putting on a virtual-reality headset that allows you to see yourself in first person in the dream situation of your choice. Spend some time exploring your experience in this environment. When feeling ready, remove your virtual headset by opening your eyes. Self-reflect and answer the following questions:

What did you see? How did you move?

_____

_____

_____

How did your body feel?

_____

_____

What were you thinking about?

_____

_____

_____

What was your emotional state?

_____

_____

What was the experience like as you aligned with your values?

_____

_____

_____

Begin by thinking about who you are without stress, then answer the following questions.

How does my body feel?

_____

_____

_____

_____

What kind of thoughts do I have?

_____

_____

_____

_____

What are the predominant emotions that arise?

_____

_____

_____

_____

How do they align with my heartfelt principles?

_____

_____

_____

_____

Now, imagine a situation where you could be experiencing this in real life. While seated with your eyes closed, picture yourself putting on a virtual-reality headset that allows you to see yourself in first person in the dream situation of your choice. Spend some time exploring your experience in this environment. When feeling ready, remove your virtual headset by opening your eyes. Self-reflect and answer the following questions:

What did you see? How did you move?

_____

_____

_____

How did your body feel?

_____

_____

What were you thinking about?

_____

_____

_____

What was your emotional state?

_____

_____

What was the experience like as you aligned with your values?

_____

_____

_____

Begin by thinking about who you are without stress, then answer the following questions.

How does my body feel?

_____

_____

_____

_____

What kind of thoughts do I have?

_____

_____

_____

_____

What are the predominant emotions that arise?

_____

_____

_____

_____

How do they align with my heartfelt principles?

_____

_____

_____

_____

Now, imagine a situation where you could be experiencing this in real life. While seated with your eyes closed, picture yourself putting on a virtual-reality headset that allows you to see yourself in first person in the dream situation of your choice. Spend some time exploring your experience in this environment. When feeling ready, remove your virtual headset by opening your eyes. Self-reflect and answer the following questions:

What did you see? How did you move?

_____

_____

_____

How did your body feel?

_____

_____

What were you thinking about?

_____

_____

_____

What was your emotional state?

_____

_____

What was the experience like as you aligned with your values?

_____

_____

_____

Begin by thinking about who you are without stress, then answer the following questions.

How does my body feel?

_____

_____

_____

_____

What kind of thoughts do I have?

_____

_____

_____

_____

What are the predominant emotions that arise?

_____

_____

_____

_____

How do they align with my heartfelt principles?

_____

_____

_____

_____

Now, imagine a situation where you could be experiencing this in real life. While seated with your eyes closed, picture yourself putting on a virtual-reality headset that allows you to see yourself in first person in the dream situation of your choice. Spend some time exploring your experience in this environment. When feeling ready, remove your virtual headset by opening your eyes. Self-reflect and answer the following questions:

What did you see? How did you move?

_____

_____

_____

How did your body feel?

_____

_____

What were you thinking about?

_____

_____

_____

What was your emotional state?

_____

_____

What was the experience like as you aligned with your values?

_____

_____

_____

Begin by thinking about who you are without stress, then answer the following questions.

How does my body feel?

_____

_____

_____

_____

What kind of thoughts do I have?

_____

_____

_____

_____

What are the predominant emotions that arise?

_____

_____

_____

_____

How do they align with my heartfelt principles?

_____

_____

_____

_____

Now, imagine a situation where you could be experiencing this in real life. While seated with your eyes closed, picture yourself putting on a virtual-reality headset that allows you to see yourself in first person in the dream situation of your choice. Spend some time exploring your experience in this environment. When feeling ready, remove your virtual headset by opening your eyes. Self-reflect and answer the following questions:

What did you see? How did you move?

_____

_____

_____

How did your body feel?

_____

_____

What were you thinking about?

_____

_____

_____

What was your emotional state?

_____

_____

What was the experience like as you aligned with your values?

_____

_____

_____

Begin by thinking about who you are without stress, then answer the following questions.

How does my body feel?

_____

_____

_____

_____

What kind of thoughts do I have?

_____

_____

_____

_____

What are the predominant emotions that arise?

_____

_____

_____

_____

How do they align with my heartfelt principles?

_____

_____

_____

_____

Now, imagine a situation where you could be experiencing this in real life. While seated with your eyes closed, picture yourself putting on a virtual-reality headset that allows you to see yourself in first person in the dream situation of your choice. Spend some time exploring your experience in this environment. When feeling ready, remove your virtual headset by opening your eyes. Self-reflect and answer the following questions:

What did you see? How did you move?

_____

_____

_____

How did your body feel?

_____

_____

What were you thinking about?

_____

_____

_____

What was your emotional state?

_____

_____

What was the experience like as you aligned with your values?

_____

_____

_____

Begin by thinking about who you are without stress, then answer the following questions.

How does my body feel?

_____

_____

_____

_____

What kind of thoughts do I have?

_____

_____

_____

_____

What are the predominant emotions that arise?

_____

_____

_____

_____

How do they align with my heartfelt principles?

_____

_____

_____

_____

Now, imagine a situation where you could be experiencing this in real life. While seated with your eyes closed, picture yourself putting on a virtual-reality headset that allows you to see yourself in first person in the dream situation of your choice. Spend some time exploring your experience in this environment. When feeling ready, remove your virtual headset by opening your eyes. Self-reflect and answer the following questions:

What did you see? How did you move?

_____

_____

_____

How did your body feel?

_____

_____

What were you thinking about?

_____

_____

_____

What was your emotional state?

_____

_____

What was the experience like as you aligned with your values?

_____

_____

_____

Inspiring | Educating | Creating | Entertaining

Brimming with creative inspiration, how-to projects, and useful information to enrich your everyday life, quarto.com is a favorite destination for those pursuing their interests and passions.

© 2021 by Charlene Rymsha

First published in 2021 by Rock Point, an imprint of The Quarto Group, 142 West 36th Street, 4th Floor, New York, NY 10018, USA
T (212) 779-4972 F (212) 779-6058 www.Quarto.com

All rights reserved. No part of this journal may be reproduced in any form without written permission of the copyright owners. All images in this journal have been reproduced with the knowledge and prior consent of the artists concerned, and no responsibility is accepted by producer, publisher, or printer for any infringement of copyright or otherwise, arising from the contents of this publication. Every effort has been made to ensure that credits accurately comply with information supplied. We apologize for any inaccuracies that may have occurred and will resolve inaccurate or missing information in a subsequent reprinting of the journal.

Rock Point titles are also available at discount for retail, wholesale, promotional, and bulk purchase. For details, contact the Special Sales Manager by email at specialsales@quarto.com or by mail at The Quarto Group, Attn: Special Sales Manager, 100 Cummings Center Suite 265D, Beverly, MA 01915 USA.

10 9 8 7 6 5 4 3

ISBN: 978-1-63106-818-8

Publisher: Rage Kindelsperger
Creative Director: Laura Drew
Managing Editor: Cara Donaldson
Senior Editor: Katharine Moore
Interior Design: Kim Winscher

Printed in China

This book provides general information on various widely known and widely accepted self-care and wellness practices. However, it should not be relied upon as recommending or promoting any specific diagnosis or method of treatment for a particular condition, and it is not intended as a substitute for medical advice or for direct diagnosis and treatment of a medical condition by a qualified physician. Readers who have questions about a particular condition, possible treatments for that condition, or possible reactions from the condition or its treatment should consult a physician or other qualified healthcare professional.